NANABUSH TALES
AND
OTHER STORIES

WINTER STORIES

—

RICHARD NANAWIN

RICHARD NANAWIN
Nanabush Tales and Other Stories
Winter Stories

F

Copyright © 2023 by Richard Nanawin

All rights reserved. No part of this publication may be reproduced, stored or transmitted in any form or by any means, electronic, mechanical, photocopying, recording, scanning, or otherwise without written permission from the publisher. It is illegal to copy this book, post it to a website, or distribute it by any other means without permission.

This novel is entirely a work of fiction. The names, characters and incidents portrayed in it are the work of the author's imagination. Any resemblance to actual persons, living or dead, events or localities is entirely coincidental.

Richard Nanawin asserts the moral right to be identified as the author of this work.

Richard Nanawin has no responsibility for the persistence or accuracy of URLs for external or third-party Internet Websites referred to in this publication and does not guarantee that any content on such Websites is, or will remain, accurate or appropriate.

Designations used by companies to distinguish their products are often claimed as trademarks. All brand names and product names used in this book and on its cover are trade names, service marks, trademarks and registered trademarks of their respective owners. The publishers and the book are not associated with any product or vendor mentioned in this book. None of the companies referenced within the book have endorsed the book.

Second edition

ISBN: 978-1-7773352-0-5

Advisor: Richard George

This book was professionally typeset on Reedsy. Find out more at reedsy.com

To my wife Sherri and my children Alexander, Taylor Rae, Kalib and Ciara

"For everyone who's finished a book under their covers with a flashlight when they were supposed to be sleeping"

ANONYMOUS

Contents

Foreword	iii
Preface	iv
Contents	vi
How the Porcupine (Gaag) got its Quills (Gaaway)	vii
The Story of Raccoon (Esiban)	x
The Moose (Mooz), the Horse Fly (Mizizaak) and the Lakes...	xiii
Nanabush and the Geese (Nika)	xvii
Nanabush, the Rose (Oginiiwaatig) and the Rabbit (Waabooz)	xxi
Nanabush and the Maple Tree (Aninaatig)	xxvi
Nanabush and Wild Rice (Manoomin)	xxix
Nanabush and the Great Flood (Mooshka'an)	xxxii
How Chipmunk (Agongosens) got his Stripes	xxxviii
How the Birch Tree (Omaaîmitig) got its Scars	xlii
The White Birch Tree (Wiigwaasaatig)	xliv
Indian Corn (Anishinaabe Mandaaminaak)	xlviii
How the Turtle (Mishekae) got its Shell	lv
Nanabush Gets Power from the Skunk (Shaagaak)	lviii
Nanabush Creates the M'Chigeeng Bluffs	lxi
The Fox (Waagosh) and the Bear (Makwa)	lxiv
Nanabush and Dog (Animosh)	lxix
Why People (Anishinaabe) do not live forever	lxxii
Nanabush and Rude Eagle (Migizi)	lxxv

Nanabush and the Woodpecker (Baapaase)	lxxvii
The Great Spirit (Gitchi Manitou), the Rabbit (Waabooz) and...	lxxxi
Nanabush and the Great Beaver (Amik)	lxxxiv
About the Author	2

Foreword

Richard Nanawin
**LIBRARY AND ARCHIVES CANADA CATALOGING
IN PUBLICATION**
Nanawin, Richard, 1965-author
Nanabush Tales and Other Stories
ISBN 978-1-7773352-0-5
eBook ISBN 978-1-7773352-0-5

Preface

For most of my life, I have listened to and retold Nanabush stories to my children around the campfire; my daughter Ciara followed along closely and began retelling the stories to her friends. I enjoy retelling the stories. First, however, my daughter insisted I start to write them all down, a task that took many years to complete.

Ojibwe Legends were passed down through generations, usually told by Ojibwe Gichi-Anishinaabe around the fire (ishkode) during the long winter (biboon) seasons. Each generation retold the stories with their general interpretation; all lead back to the seven grandfather teachings of respect, honesty, truth, humility, courage, wisdom and love.

Nanabush, the trickster, is a likeable character who dispenses advice all while getting into situations all his own making. Along the way, Nanabush helps his Grandmother (Nokomis) and the Animals (Awesiinh) of Turtle Island (Mishekae) live better lives.

I began writing down the first stories in the fall of 2012 and have continued over the years as time allowed; it is the summer of 2020 the time has come to publish.

It is my wish that all ages enjoy Nanabush Tales and Other Stories and share them with family and friends around the campfire.

Miigwetch,

Richard Nanawin

Contents

1. How the Porcupine got its Quills
2. The Story of Raccoon
3. The Moose, the Horse Fly, and the Lakes
4. Nanabush and the Geese
5. Nanabush, the Rose and the Rabbit
6. Nanabush and the Maple Tree
7. Nanabush and Wild Rice
8. Nanabush and the Great Flood
9. How Chipmunk got his Stripes
10. How the White Birch Tree got its scars
11. The White Birch Tree
12. Indian Corn
13. How the Turtle got it's Shell
14. Nanabush receives power from the Skunk
15. Nanabush Creates the M'Chigeeng Bluffs
16. The Fox and the Bear
17. Nanabush and Dog Tails
18. Why People don't live forever
19. Nanabush and the Rude Eagle
20. Gitchi Manitou, the Rabbit and the Owl
21. Nanabush, Grandmother and the Great Beaver

How the Porcupine (Gaag) got its Quills (Gaaway)

Porcupine (Gaag)

A long time ago, Porcupines (Gaag) had no Quills (Gaaway). So he had to be very careful when eating. Much larger animals liked to eat Porcupines (Gaag). One day Porcupine(Gaag) was out eating and heard a noise. He noticed Bear (Makwa) running towards him. He quickly climbed a tree. Bear (Makwa) could not reach him and was safe for now.

The next day Porcupine (Gaag) returned to the forest to eat. He noticed some ground berries near a thorn bush (mazaanaatig). He crawled under the thorn bush (mazaanaatig) to get the berries. Unfortunately, the thorns on the low branches scratched and poked his tender skin.

He managed to crawl close enough to eat some berries. While eating the berries, he had an idea. He chewed through some low branches and placed them on his back. He was careful not to poke himself with the thorn bush branches (mazaanaatig).

Later that afternoon, he went out to eat again and saw Bear (Makwa) coming towards him. He froze in his tracks. The Great Bear (Makwa) tried to bite him. The thorn bush branches (mazaanaatig) pierced the Great Bear's (Makwa's) mouth. He let out a tremendous roar. Then, he ran into the nearby trees with thorn bush branches (mazaanaatig) stuck in his mouth.

Nanabush (the Trickster) was nearby and watched with curiosity. He was amazed by the Porcupine (Gaag), and his thorn bush branches (mazaanaatig) covered back. So Nanabush walked over to the Porcupine (Gaag). Nanabush said, "I will use his powers to make sure you could always have thorn bush branches (mazaanaatig) to protect yourself.

Nanabush went to the thorn bush (mazaanaatig) and removed many thorn bush branches (mazaanaatig). He peeled back the bark exposing the white underlayer. He grabbed some wet white clay from the nearby shore and carefully coated each one. Nanabush gently placed each thorn bush branch (mazaanaatig) row upon row on the Porcupine's (Gaag's) back. He told Porcupine (Gaag) to rest and let the thorn bush branches (mazaanaatig) dry.

The following day Porcupine (Gaag) awoke to find the thorn bush branches (mazaanaatig) had dried. Porcupines (Gaag) now had hundreds of brilliant white thorn bush branches (mazaanaatig) lying flat row upon row on its back. Porcupine (Gaag) decided he was hungry. So he went down to the river to eat some grass. Porcupine (Gaag) spotted Wolf (Ma'iingan) coming towards him. Porcupine (Gaag) rolled into a ball just as Wolf (Ma'iingan) jumped upon him. Wolf (Ma'iingan) howled in pain as the hundreds of thorn branch bushes (mazaanaatig) pierced the Wolf's (Ma'iingan) mouth, nose, and face. Wolf (Ma'iingan) ran back into the forest, howling.

To this day, Porcupine (Gaag) can wander the forest safely with his gift of white Quills (Gaaway) from Nanabush.

The Story of Raccoon (Esiban)

Raccoon (Esiban)

Nanabush (Trickster) lived in a village. He had built two lodges (wiigiwaams), one for himself and another for two elderly brothers who were blind. Nanabush tied a rope from their lodge (wiigiwaam) to the water's edge so they could follow the string to get water when needed. One day Raccoon (Esiban) decided to play a trick on the brothers. He saw the one brother coming down the path to fetch water. Raccoon (Esiban) quickly untied the rope and threw it near the trees.

When the brother got to the rope's end, he discovered no water. Raccoon (Esiban) laughed. The brother returned to the lodge (wiigiwaam) and said he could not find the water. The other brother took the pail and followed the rope to the edge of the great lake (Gichigami). Raccoon (Esiban) saw the other brother coming. He quickly grabbed the rope and placed it back in the water. Brother found the water, retrieved some and walked back to the lodge.

When the brother returned, he said, "Your lazy brother, you wanted me to get the water" the other brother replied, "I could not find the water. I'm glad you did. Let's have some tea." As the brothers sat down to drink their tea, Nanabush entered their wiigiwaam and announced he'd brought them some fresh deer stew and corn. The brothers were pleased. Nanabush ensured each brother had two pieces of deer meat in each bowl.

Raccoon (Esiban) had smelled the deer stew and followed Nanabush to the brother's lodge (wiigiwaam). After Nanabush left, Raccoon (Esiban) crept up upon the table and took the deer meat from one brother's bowl. Then, he hurried to the corner of the lodge (wiigiwaam), where he quickly enjoyed his fresh deer meat. As the brothers began to eat, one brother said, "Your greedy brother, you've taken my deer meat" the other brother exclaimed," I have done no such thing; Nanabush gave us two pieces each."

While the brothers were arguing, Esiban crept up on the table and took the last two pieces of deer meat. He gleefully ran to the corner of the lodge (wiigiwaam) and enjoyed his deer meat. When the brothers resumed eating, the other brother yelled," You took my deer meat, "the other brother yelled back," I did not!! You must've eaten them already." The brothers began to yell louder and began to wrestle and fight. Raccoon (Esiban) was incredibly happy to watch the brothers fight.

Nanabush heard the yelling and ran to the lodge (wiigiwaam) to find the two-brothers wrestling on the floor. The Raccoon (Esiban) saw Nanabush coming and tried to leave the lodge (wiigiwaam) without being seen. Nanabush saw Raccoon and grabbed him by the scuff, "What have you been up to?" Nanabush listened to the brother's story. He was angered by Raccoon's (Esiban's) behaviour and the troubles he had caused the brothers.

Nanabush decided the world would know of Raccoon's (Esiban's) misery. He told Raccoon (Esiban), "I am going to take away half your eyesight. You will see but not very well. You will only be able to hunt at night. When you find food, you will have to find water to wash it before eating."

Nanabush took some soot from the fire (ishkode) and rubbed it across Raccoon's (Esiban's) face. Then, he took more and wiped it across Raccoon's tale. "From now on, people will see your mask and know to be wary of you. The four stripes on your tail will remind you of the meat you took from the brothers."

The Moose (Mooz), the Horse Fly (Mizizaak) and the Lakes (Aanikegamaa)

Moose (Mooz)

Many years ago, a great lake (Gichigami) covered much of Turtle Island (mishekae). All the Animals (Awesiinh) shared the great lake (Gichigami) for its freshwater and abundance of fish. Then, one day a great Moose (Mooz) appeared at the edge of the great lake (Gichigami). He drank the water incredibly, so much so that the great lake (Gichigami) level began to drop.

The next day, the Moose (Mooz) returned and began to drink again. But, unfortunately, his thirst was slowly draining the great lake (Gichigami). This worried the Beavers (Amik). The water around their lodges (amikwiish) was draining away, exposing their underwater entrances.

Many of the other Animals (Awesiinh), like the Muskrat (Wazhashk), Fish (Giigoonh) and Birds (Bineshiinh), were also worried. The Moose (Mooz) would drain the great lake (Gichigami) they depended upon for a living.

The Moose (Mooz) continued to drink every day. The great lake (Gichigami) water level was getting very low. Some Animals (Awesiinh) could eat on land but not the Fish (Giigoonh) in the great lake (Gichigami). So the Animals (Awesiinh) came together. They all agreed they needed to drive the Moose (Mooz) away from the great lake (Gichigami). They feared him, including the Great Bear (Makwa).

While the Animals (Awesiinh) were deciding what to do, a small Horsefly (Mizizaak) came to a circle. He said he would drive the Moose (Mooz) away. Some Animals (Awesiinh) were amazed at his bravery, but many laughed out loud.

The small horse fly (Mizizaak) flew away. He could be heard saying, "You'll see, you'll see what I can do." The very next day, the Moose (Mooz) appeared on the shore of the great lake (Gichigami). He began drinking the water. The Horsefly (Mizizaak) spotted him and flew toward the leg of the Moose (Mooz). Horsefly (Mizizaak) found a soft spot and bit down as hard as possible. The Moose (Mooz) stamped his hoof and tried to shake off the irritating Horsefly (Mizizaak).

The Horsefly (Mizizaak) flew up and landed behind the ear of the Moose (Mooz). He bit down again. This time the Moose (Mooz) stomped furiously, making great holes with his stomping hooves. Each time the Horsefly (Mizizaak) bit down, the Moose (Mooz) would stamp, creating large holes which filled quickly with water. The Horsefly (Mizizaak) flew around the Moose (Mooz), and he bit him repeatedly. Finally, the Moose (Mooz) was getting angry. He ran up the shoreline towards the trees stomping, water filling each great hole he left behind.

Horsefly (Mizizaak) did not give up. The Moose (Mooz) shook his head, stomping and running in circles snorting and blowing. The Animals (Awesiinh) on the other shoreline watched as the Horsefly (Mizizaak) flew bravely around the great Mooz. But, unfortunately, he continued to bite him repeatedly.

The Moose (Mooz) tried with all his might, but he could shake off biting Horsefly (Mizizaak). Finally, the Moose (Mooz) could not take it anymore. He ran off, stomping back towards the northern territory he came from. The Moose (Mooz) had made thousands of holes with all the stamping, thrashing, and running about. Each one filled with water as the Moose(Mooz) ran northward.

Today, much of Turtle Island (Mishekae) has thousands of great lakes (Gichigami) thanks to Mizizaak and the great Mooz. When the great Mooz returned home, he told his story about the terrible Mizizaaks in the south; today, most Mooz lives in the north. The Mizizaak was immensely proud of his work; he had saved the great lake (Gichigami) and the future generations of awesiinh.

The awesiinh were very gracious; they promised the Horsefly

(Mizizaak) that, should any animal die of old age or disease, the Horsefly (Mizizaak) might have the entire body to feed and lay their eggs for future generations.

Nanabush and the Geese (Nika)

Geese (Nika)

One day Nanabush was wandering near the great lake (Gichigami)) when he spotted some Geese (Nika) feeding near the shore. He was hungry and decided he would catch a few to eat. As he approached the great lake (Gichigami), the Geese (Nika) spotted Nanabush and swam further from shore. Nanabush had to get closer without scaring his meal away.

Nanabush had some basswood rope (wiigob biiminakwaan)

with him, but he needed to go underwater to get closer. He saw some tall reeds (anaakanashk) a little down the shore. So Nanabush wandered down the shoreline, broke off a long piece of tall reed (anaakanashk) and sank beneath the water using the tall reed (anaakanashk) to breathe.

As he swam towards the Geese (Nika), he could see their webbed feet paddling around. They were unaware that Nanabush was beneath them. Nanabush counted at least 12 pairs of webbed feet. He decided he'd slip knots (gashka'oozh) around one foot on each goose (Nika). He completed his task without the Geese (Nika) realizing what was happening beneath them.

After he was done, he tied the ends of the basswood rope (wiigob biiminakwaan) to each of his hands. Then, he leapt out of the water and gave a mighty tug on the string. The Geese (Nika) was startled and took the air flapping wildly and honking to warn others. As the Nika took the air, the rope (gashka'oozh) on their feet tightened. Nanabush gave another great pull to capture his dinner. The Geese (Nika) flew higher and higher. Nanabush was being dragged across the great lake (Gichigami), and then suddenly, he was above the great lake (Gichigami), rising towards the sky.

Nanabush soon realized he was in trouble. All the Geese (Nika) were tied together (gashka'oodoon) and flying higher and higher. Nanabush began to yell, "Let me down, let me down!!" The Geese (Nika) flew high over the great lake (Gichigami). They were headed toward the marsh (waabashkiki) at the other end. One of the Geese (Nika) yelled back, "Cut us loose; the marsh (waabashkiki) will catch you!!" Nanabush pulled out his knife and cut one hand loose, then the other. He was suddenly falling towards the marsh (waabashkiki). He landed with a great splash but was not hurt.

Nanabush was wet and disappointed his plan did not work. He stared towards the sky and saw the Geese (Nika) landing in the neighbouring great lake (Gichigami) still tied together (gashka'oodoon). He walked towards the great lake (Gichigami) and saw Nika close to shore. They were angry. One said, "What were you trying to do, Nanabush" he smiled and replied, "I just wanted to fly." The Geese (Nika were still angry, but one said, "Untie us, and we'll show you how to fly," Nanabush thought for a moment, "Dinner could wait; learning to fly would be most enjoyable." Nanabush carefully untied his basswood rope (wiigob biiminakwaan) from each Geese (Nika). They were grateful and told Nanabush to run alongside them on the shoreline as they took to the sky again.

As the Geese (Nika) took to the sky one by one, Nanabush ran down the shoreline as fast as he could to keep up. Suddenly, his feet were no longer on the ground. One of the Geese (Nika) could be heard, "Don't look down, don't look down!!", Nanabush listened. He rose into the air, flapping his arms, and soared with the Geese (Nika).

Nanabush could see many of the Animals (Awesiinh) on the mountains (wajiw) up ahead. So he decided he would wave to them as he flew by. So as the Geese (Nika) approached the mountain (wajiw), Nanabush took one of his hands and waved to the Animals (Awesiinh) on the mountaintop (wajiw).

Nanabush suddenly realized he was falling toward the trees (mitig). He flapped harder, but this did nothing to stop his fall to the earth. Nanabush crashed in the treetops (wanakong) and bounced across the tree branches before coming to a tumbling stop under a pine tree.

A couple of the Nika landed nearby. They told Nanabush he

should not have looked down. He would still be soaring in the sky. Nanabush was hungry and bruised. He soon realized his waving to show off caused his fall.

To this day, Geese (Nika) fly in a perfect V shape like they are tied together (gashka'oodoon).

Nanabush, the Rose (Oginiiwaatig) and the Rabbit (Waabooz)

Many years ago, the meadows and river valleys were covered in wild rose bushes (Oginiiwaatig). There among the wild rose bushes (Oginiiwaatig) were wild dandelions, berries aplenty, and many Hummingbird (Nanookaasi) flying and buzzing from wild rose bush (Oginiiwaatig) to wild rose bush (Oginiiwaatig).

The Hummingbird (Nanookaasi), the Bees (Amookaa) and other insects were busily sucking the sweet nectar from the wild rose bush (Oginiiwaatig) flowers. The Bees (Amookaas) work energetically to fill their honeycombs for the coming winter season. There were many honeycombs for everyone. The Great Bear (Makwa) and the other Animals (Awesiinh) helped themselves, eating what they wanted and growing fat for their winter (biboon) sleep. The wild rose bush (Oginiiwaatig) was very important. Many Animals (Awesiinh) depended upon the wild rose bush (Oginiiwaatig) for the nectar, especially the Bees (Amookaas) who made the honey.

Over time, many of the Animals (Awesiinh) became accustomed to the plentiful feast offered by mother earth, and some Animals (Awesiinh) started to become greedy. One day, many rabbits (Waabooz) were out looking for food, their stomachs were empty, and they were hungry.

One noticed a big patch of wild rose bushes (Oginiiwaatig) and ran towards the brightly coloured flowers. Many others followed and began to nibble on the rose petals. The petals were overly sweet; a feast had begun.

Before long, all the Rabbits (Waabooz) ate the rose petals wherever they found a wild rose bush (Oginiiwaatig). They could be heard saying, "We love rose petals; there sweet; no more grass and clover for us." The Rabbits (Waabooz) continued to feast as spring turned to summer, growing fat. Other Animals (Awesiinh), like the deer, joined the feast. It did not take for the other Animals (Awesiinh) to notice that all that was left were the stems and leaves.

As time passed, the Great Bear Makwa noticed that their honeycombs were not as plentiful as they once were. So the Bees

(Amookaa) complained to the Hummingbird (Nanookaasi).

The Hummingbird (Nanookaasi) said, "We're hungry, too!! There's little nectar for us!! The wild rose bushes (Oginiiwaatig) are gone!!" Summer passed into autumn, and the beginnings of the winter (biboon) season was upon the forest Animal (Awesiinh). The Great Bear (Makwa) and her family began to go to their winter (biboon) dens for their long sleep. The Great Bear (Makwa's) children ask, "Will there be more honeycomb next year," Mother Bear (Makwa) says, "Yes, there will be wild rose bushes (Oginiiwaatig) covering the hills. So much clover, dandelions and berries with lots of nectar for all; rest now, little ones." Throughout the winter (biboon), the Great Bear (Makwa) and the other Animals (Awesiinh) dreamt of spring berries, wild rose bushes (Oginiiwaatig) and fresh nectar.

When spring arrived, the Oginiiwaatig burst into bloom, their flowers blossomed, and the nectar began to flow. The Waabooz was the first to notice; they moved fast and began to eat all the rose petals near their hutches. This wasn't enough for the Waabooz; they crossed the valley meadow and searched out every Oginiiwaatig; they ate all the petals, leaving behind only the stem and leaves. They grew fatter and fatter, consuming all they could find throughout the valleys and hills.

The other awesiinh was getting worried; Makwa called a meeting of the awesiinh kingdom, "Where has all the honeycomb gone!!" Then, another Makwa shouted, "There's not enough honeycomb for us!!" "We don't know," said the Amookaa, "there's not enough nectar."

"The sweet nectar has run out," said the Hummingbird.

As the awesiinh mulled over the honeycomb and the nectar's loss, Makwa noticed all the awesiinh were skinny except for all the fat Waabooz.

"Look how fat the Waabooz are!! They have eaten all the rose petals!! He bellowed out loud. The other awesiinh became mad and set upon all the Waabooz, yelling and pulling their ears.

"Stop, stop, please," one rabbit said; the flailing continued; the Waabooz were likely to be driven to the mountains where roses are not abundant; they were afraid.

Nanabush, the trickster, had Amookaan sent by the creator Gitchi Manitou to look after all the creatures of mishekae Island. Nanabush could hear the Waabooz screams; he went towards the valley and saw what was happening. He thundered, "Stop hurting the Waabooz, all of you!! The awesiinh stopped and were frightened; they did not expect to hear the voice of Nanabush.

Makwa said, "The Waabooz have eaten all the Oginiiwaatig, the Amookaas have little nectar for honeycomb, the Nanookaasi have little food, and the Waabooz are fat with greed."

Nanabush said, "Not all the Oginiiwaatig are gone; follow me," he said. So the awesiinh followed Nanabush down an unfamiliar trail; suddenly, a clearing appeared. In the middle were a glorious garden of Oginiiwaatig, berry bushes, clover blooms, and wonderful scent.

Nanabush said, "Waabooz, you're welcome to my Ogini-iwaatig; eat at your heart's content" The Waabooz eagerly jumped, hopped and ran towards the Oginiiwaatig in Nanabush's garden.

Makwa looked confused. "No, Nanabush, they will eat all your Oginiiwaatig." Nanabush smiled and reassured Makwa, "Don't worry so much."

All the Waabooz set upon the Oginiiwaatig in a petal-eating frenzy, ears straight back and noses are quivering with the sweet smells.

Suddenly, they were hundreds of screams; all the Waabooz were running back, their pink noses all bleeding from little holes.

Nanabush laughed, "Thorns plenty; I gave every Oginiiwaatig hundreds of thorns to protect them from your greed; the roses will always bloom, the nectar will always flow."

Since all roses have thorns, Waabooz's ears are long from being stretched; they do not dare go near wild roses.

Nanabush and the Maple Tree (Aninaatig)

Aninaatig

When Turtle (Mishekae) Island was new, Great Spirit (Gitchi Manitou) made life very easy for the People (Anishinaabe) long ago. There was plenty of game, the weather was always good, and the Maple Trees (Aninaatig) were filled with a sweet thick syrup. Whenever anyone wanted to get Maple Syrup

(Zhiiwaagamizigan) from the trees, they had to break off a twig and collect it as it dripped out.

One day, Nanabush went walking around. "I think I'll go see how my friends, the People (Anishinaabe), are doing," he said. Nanabush went to a village of the Ojibwe people; there was no one around; Nanabush looked for the people (Anishinaabe). They were not fishing in the streams or the lake. They were not working in the fields with their crops. They were not gathering berries. Finally, he found them. They were in the grove of Maple Trees (Aninaatig) near the village; the people were lying on their backs with their mouths open, letting Maple Syrup (Zhiiwaagamizigan) drip into their mouths.

"This will not do!" Nanabush said. "My people (Anishinaabe) will all be fat and lazy if they keep living this way." So, Nanabush went down to the river. He took with him a big basket he had made of birch bark. With this basket, he brought back many buckets of water. Then, he went to the top of the Maple Tree (Aninaatig) and poured water to thin out the Maple Syrup (Zhiiwaagamizigan)

Now, thick Maple Syrup (Zhiiwaagamizigan) no longer dripped out of the broken twigs. Now what came out was thin, watery, and just barely sweet.

"This is how it will be from now on," Nanabush said. "No longer will syrup drip from the Maple Tree (Aninaatig). Now there will only be this watery sap. So then, when people (Anishinaabe) want to make Maple Syrup (Zhiiwaagamizigan), they will gather many buckets full of liquid in birch bark baskets like mine.

They will have to gather wood and make a Fire (Ishkode) to heat stones to drop into the baskets. They will have to boil the water with the heated stones for a long time to make even a little

Maple Syrup (Zhiiwaagamizigan). My people (Anishinaabe) will no longer grow fat and lazy. They will appreciate this Maple Syrup (Zhiiwaagamizigan) and The Great Spirit (Gitchi Manitou) made available to them. Not only that, but this Maple Syrup (Zhiiwaagamizigan) will drip only from the trees at a particular time of the year. Then it will not keep people from hunting, fishing, gathering, and looking after the fields.

"This is how it is going to be," Nanabush said. And that is how it is to this day.

Nanabush and Wild Rice (Manoomin)

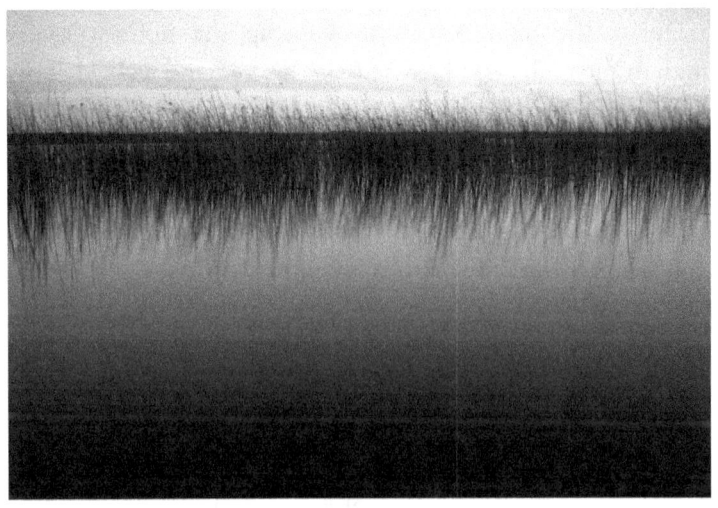

Manoomin

Nanabush was worried about what his people would eat during the long winter (biboon) months ahead; there had been extraordinarily little food for several long winters (biboon), and the people had suffered.

Nanabush desired to help his people (anishinaabekaa); he didn't like to see them hungry (bakade), he decided to go into the woods (jekaakwa'am) and fast for five days in a wigwam he built. On the morning of the fifth day, Nanabush went for a long walk; as he walked further into the forest, his thoughts returned to how people went hungry. Nanabush walked for a very long time; he came to the edge of a great lake (Gichigami); it was very late, and he was exhausted, so he laid to rest and fell asleep.

During the night, Nanabush woke up; the moon was very high in the night sky; he rose from his bed and walked along the river; he saw what looked like dancers on the water(nibi).

Nanabush noticed the dancer's headdresses looked like those worn by Ojibwe men. Nanabush walked closer to the dancers and asked if he could dance with them. Nanabush danced and danced under the moonlit night sky; he grew tired, lay down, and fell asleep. When Nanabush woke up in the morning, everything was calm; he remembered the dancers but thought it all had been a dream.

As Nanabush looked out over the great lake (Gichigami), he saw tassels waving in the wind close to the lakeshore. So Nanabush walked into the great lake; he found long seeds(miinikaan) hanging from the tassels. Nanabush gathered some of these seeds in his hand's palm and carried them back to his wigwam.

Nanabush continued fasting; he grew tired and fell asleep again; as he slept, he had another dream. He learned that the seeds he had gathered could be boiled and eaten as food in his dream. Nanabush put some seeds in his mouth; they tasted good. Then, Nanabush returned to the village, told his people about the roots, and encouraged them to collect as much as possible before winter (biboon).

Together, they harvested enough to provide wild rice for the long biboon.

Nanabush and the Great Flood
(Mooshka'an)

great lake (Gichigami)

A long time ago, Gichi Manitou, the great spirit, dreamt of creating mountains (wajiw), valleys, forests with plentiful rivers, and many animals and birds. After waking, Gichi Manitou decided to make his dream a reality; he began creating his world (miziwekamig).

Gichi Manitou created the sun to give light and warmth to his new world; it would provide the energy to grow and heal plants, animals and humans. He made great lakes and rivers to renew and purify the soil and created wind to offer the first breath of life for all. Finally, Gichi Manitou created humans and gave them the power to dream of new futures and renew memories. Humans were young and needed help in their new world; Gichi Manitou decided he would send Nanabush (the Trickster), the moon's grandson and the west wind's son would teach humans to survive to learn some valuable lessons of his own. Nanabush was the oldest brother; his younger brothers were lazy; he spent much time reminding them to be careful.

Nanabush and his brothers enjoyed the companionship of birds and beasts, but there was one enemy in this world. These were the Serpent People. One winter day, one of Nanabush's brothers went out to hunt, but when he had not returned by the following day, Nanabush realized something was wrong. He had warned his brothers never to walk across the frozen lake, but he suspected this brother had disobeyed him.

All that winter, Nanabush searched for his brother (nisayenh), but he became increasingly convinced the Serpent People had drowned him as time passed. They had the power to live beneath the frozen lake for months at a time, and if they had taken his brother there, he would not survive. Then, at long last, one day, he heard a loud booming sound. He scrambled to the top of a hill to see what he could see, and what he saw amazed him. Spring had come, and there, in the valley below, beside a lake, lay two Serpent People sunning themselves. The booming sound was only the beating of their hearts.

Anger (biijigidaazo) welled up in Nanabush when he saw them, for he knew they had stolen his brother. So he drew his bow and shot an arrow into each serpent, and though the arrows hit their marks, the serpents slipped into the melting lake and disappeared. Moments later, the water in that little lake began to rise, and the whole valley was flooded before long.

Now Nanabush understood. The Serpent People meant to drown him too. Quickly he climbed to the top of the tallest pine tree, but the water continued to rise. Soon it was near his feet, growing still, and then a peculiar thing happened as it reached his chin. The water began to recede, draining away as quickly as it had risen. Nanabush knew he had been warned. When the floodwaters were gone, Nanabush climbed down from the top of the tree and began to take down the trees around him.

He built a giant raft with these trees, which he left at the top of the highest hill. Then he wandered once again into the valley below. Suddenly he saw a woman on a log. She was weeping. "What's wrong?" Nanabush asked as he approached her.

"The wicked Nanabush has wounded my brothers," the woman cried. Now Nanabush understood this was a serpent woman, but she did not recognize him. "Ah, that trickster," Nanabush said, "he cannot be trusted; allow me to help you." "I am gathering basswood bark and making a string," she said. "When Nanabush walks this way, he will trip the string, and when we see the vibrations, we'll know where he is; we shall kill him." "Where do you live?" asked Nanabush. "I will go help tend to your brothers."

"Down this path," she said. "When you reach the lake, walk right in, and there you will find a door. Behind that door are my people." "Until later," Nanabush called, moving swiftly into the lake, transforming himself as he moved into a serpent woman.

When he found the door, he opened it and entered an enormous wiigiwaam. There lay the two wounded serpents, arrows still piercing their skin. Many other fierce creatures guarded them, but they were in a far corner; Nanabush saw his brother. And it was true; his brother had been drowned. Nanabush leaped forward and pushed the arrows deep into the two serpents. A moment later, they were dead. "I have paid you for my brother's death!" Nanabush cried, and before the other creatures could recognize who this intruder was, he was gone. The guardians roared. Soon they caused the lake to rise again.

But this time, Nanabush was ready. He raced to his raft, calling to every creature as he ran. "Come to my raft, climb aboard." And so, they did.

But the floodwaters continued to rise until every part of the world the creatures had known was covered. Nanabush and the others floated safely on their raft. For days and nights, they floated until a month had passed. Now Nanabush saw the world they had always known was drowned, and the wicked Serpent People went with it. "Maang!" he called to the loon. "You are an excellent swimmer. See if you can dive down to the Old World and bring back a lump of mud in your bill; with mud, I will create a New World."

Maang dove into the water and was gone a long time. When he finally did return, he said, "I could not reach the Old World. It was too far down." "Amik!" called Nanabush to the beaver. "You are an excellent swimmer. Will you try next?" Amik dove off and was gone even longer than Maang, but he, too, returned empty-handed. "Is there anyone else who'll try?" asked Nanabush.

A small coot, Aajigade, came swimming along and asked, "What's going on?" "Getaway, Aajigade," called one of the birds.

"We do not have time for your nonsense." Now the animals began arguing loudly. Everyone had a different plan for getting the mud, but no one could agree on whose plan they would use. For hours and hours, they argued. By and by, someone noticed that the sun was beginning to go down. They would have to put off the planning until the next day. Finally, everyone began to find their sleeping spot on the raft to rest for the night. Maang asked, "Whatever happened to that silly little Aajigade?"

Suddenly, there was shouting at the other end of the raft. Someone had noticed a small body floating in the water. Waterbirds paddled hurriedly to investigate and found that it was Aajigade. They brought his body to the raft. Nanabush lifted him, and looking in his small beak; he found a mud particle. Little Aajigade had reached the Old World and got the earth! He had given his life to do this. The other animals were ashamed of themselves for having made fun of little Aajigade. They hung their heads. They felt unfortunate.

Nanabush took Aajigade's little body and softly blew life back into him. Nanabush held him close to warm him and announced that Aajigade would always retain a place of honour among the animals from that day forward. Nanabush set Aajigade down on the water, and he swam off as though nothing had happened.

Then Nanabush took Aajigade's mud in his hands and began to shape it. Next, he commanded it to grow. As it grew, he needed a place to put it; the snapping turtle (mikinaak mishekae) came forward and said, "I have a broad back. Place it here." Nanabush put it on Mikinaak's back so that it could grow larger.

"Miigwetch, Mikinaak," said Nanabush. "From this day on, you shall be able to live in all the worlds, under the mud, in the water, and on land." The mud began to take the shape of the land. Nanabush placed some tiny enigoonsags (ants) on it. This made it start to spin and grow more. It grew and grew, and more animals stepped onto it until it was finally large enough for moose to walkabout.

Now Nanabush sent the birds (benishiyag) to fly around to survey how large the land was. He said to them, "Return to me now and again to let me know how the ground is doing. Send back your messages with songs. To this day, that is what the birds continue to do. That is also why they are called singers.

At last, Nanabush stepped onto the New World. It had become a home, a place for all the animals, insects and birds, and all living things to live in harmony.

How Chipmunk (Agongosens) got his Stripes

Agongosens

Once upon a time, when animals could talk, a great bear (Makwa) walked through the woods (megwayaak). This big, strong great Bear (Makwa) was much like other great Bear (Makwa) – he thought he was important.

"I can do anything," great Bear (Makwa) mumbled as he foraged for food. Just then, tiny Chipmunk (Agongosen) overheard him and, feeling bold, said, "Really? Are you sure?"

Of course," great Bear (Makwa) said, huffing. Then, he knocked over a massive log with his giant paw to prove it. "See, that was easy. I am the strongest of all the animals. They are all afraid of me. I can do anything."

Chipmunk (Agongosen) asked, "Can you keep the sun from rising tomorrow?" "I haven't tried that before," said great Bear (Makwa). Then, after thinking a minute, he said, "Yes. I am sure I can. I could do it." "You think so?" asked Chipmunk (Agongosen)."Yes. I am certain. I will show you tomorrow morning. There will be no sunrise." And great Bear (Makwa) looked to the east and sat down to wait for the morning.

It grew later and later, the sunset in the west, and great Bear (Makwa) waited; Chipmunk (Agongosen) went to bed, snuggled tight in his hole in his bed of leaves, and thought merrily of how great Bear (Makwa) would be disappointed in the morning. So great Bear (Makwa) waited and convinced himself of his mission.

Morning came, and the sky in the east began to lighten, just as it did every morning. Then, finally, the animals all began to wake, and the birds started chirping.

The Great Bear (Makwa) mustered all his will. "Stay in bed, Sun," said great Bear (Makwa). "You will not rise today. I, great Bear (Makwa), have said so. So, it will be."But the Sun did not listen and rose just as it always did. Great Bear (Makwa) was angry, but Chipmunk (Agongosen) laughed at him. "You're not as strong as you think," said Chipmunk (Agongosen). "The Sun is stronger than you are!"

Chipmunk's (Agongosen's) laughter got louder and louder,

and his teasing was beginning to get attention from the other animals. Chipmunk (Agongosen) was laughing with amusement, repeatedly yelling, "See great Bear (Makwa)? The Sun came up anyways! Do you see?"

As fast as a flash, great Bear (Makwa) reached out and trapped Chipmunk (Agongosen) under his massive paw. "I may not have stopped the sunrise," said great Bear (Makwa), "but you will never see the sunrise again."

Chipmunk (Agongosen) was not laughing anymore. "great Bear (Makwa), I was only teasing. You are so strong, so quick… you are the greatest of all the forest animals. So please take pity on me. It was only a joke." But great Bear (Makwa) held Chipmunk (Agongosen) to the ground.

"Great Bear (Makwa), you're right. I deserve to die for the awful things I said about you," said Chipmunk (Agongosen). "I'm ready to pay for my behaviour. Please let me say one last prayer before you eat me."

"Be quick about it," great Bear (Makwa) said. "It's time you were punished!"

"I will be as quick as I can," Chipmunk (Agongosen) said. "But I cannot breathe. Your huge, strong paw presses down on me so I can hardly squeak. If you would lift your paw a tiny bit, I could have enough breath for my prayer. Then you can eat me." The Great Bear (Makwa) lifted his paw just a tiny bit – and Chipmunk (Agongosen) jumped. He wiggled himself free and dashed for his nest. The Great Bear (Makwa) tried to catch him and swung a giant foot at him. Chipmunk (Agongosen) escaped before great Bear (Makwa) left three long scratches down his back.

To this day, all Chipmunks (Agongosens) wear pale scars down their back to remind them of the trouble that can come from making fun of another animal.

How the Birch Tree (Omaaîmitig) got its Scars

Omaaîmitig

This is the story about how the birch bark got its burns. It was wintertime (biboon), and Nanabush's Grandmother (Nokomis) called him to her. "Nanabush, come here (Omaabiizhaan!)," she called. Come here! "Omaabiizhaan!." It is cold, and we have no fire (ishkode) for warmth or to cook and prepare our food. So I ask you to find the ishkode that Thunderbird (Animikii) has in the west."

"Nokomis," Nanabush replied. "I will look for the great Thunderbird (Animikii) for you." So he disguised himself as a little Rabbit (Waabooz) and headed west looking for the fire (ishkode).

When Nanabush finally reached Thunderbird's (Animikii's) home, he asked, "Please share the warmth inside your home. I am cold and lost. I will only stay a little while, for I must be on my way."

The Thunderbird (Animikii) agreed and allowed Nanabush to enter his home. Inside, Nanabush saw the fire (ishkode) and waited until Thunderbird (Animikii) looked away. Then, Nanabush quickly rolled in the fire (ishkode) and took off running toward his home with the fire (ishkode) on his back!

Thunderbird (Animikii) flew behind Nanabush, throwing lightning flashes at him! Finally, Nanabush grew tired and yelled for someone to help him. Please help me! Please help me! Birch Tree (Omaaîmitig)," he cried.

Then the Birch Tree (Omaaîmitig) spoke. "Come, hide beside me, my brother. I will protect you."

The little Rabbit (Waabooz) hid beneath the tree while Thunderbird (Animikii) flashed and thundered, angry that Nanabush had stolen the fire (ishkode). The lightning bolts missed Nanabush every time, but they hit Birch Tree (Omaaîmitig); dark burn marks scarred the tree's white bark.

That is why the birch tree now has burn marks on its bark.

The White Birch Tree (Wiigwaasaatig)

Wiigwaasaatig

A long time ago, in an Ojibwe village, a gifted young man (oshki-inini) was the only son of a local mother (ogiin) whose husband had died recently. The young man (oshki-inini) was in his 14th year; he'd taken on his father's (oosan) role of hunting and gathering food for his mother and extended family.

The young man (oshki-inini) was generous; he was a great hunter (giiyosewman) and provided much meat for families that needed help. In addition, he would spend his spare time gathering fire (ishkode) wood for the Elders (Gichi-Anishinaabe) and bringing water up from the river daily.

As the season passed, it was very apparent this young man (oshki-inini) would be a great future leader, his generosity and caring ways made him extremely popular.

In the late summer of his 16th year, a great fire (ishkode) erupted close to his village; the clan's mothers decided to move the village across the river for safety. All the young men (oshki-inini) loaded the canoes and transported the Elders (Gichi-Anishinaabe) across the river to safety; the community was incredibly grateful for the young man's (oshki-inini) bravery in crossing the river many times.

The fire (ishkode) raged for days into weeks, the mountain (wajiw) behind the old village was barren, and nothing remained by ashes; the young men (oshki-inini) reminisced about the time he had spent hunting and gathering on the mountain.

The fire (ishkode) finally burnt out weeks later, and many villagers crossed over to see if anything had survived the fire (ishkode); nothing had, and the entire village site was ashes.

In the late fall, many villagers became extremely ill, including the young man (oshki-inini); the sickness affected the young and old, and it had no barriers or conscience.

Many villagers started to die; the young man (oshki-inini) hung on for a month or so, his body covered in blisters and sores. Finally, his mother exited her lodge (wiigiwaam) crying one night and told everyone her son (ingozis) had passed to the next life.

Her son (ingozis) had lived many lives in his young life; he helped others less fortunate, shared his bounty will everyone and taught the young boys many hunting skills. He had braved the cold river water many times to save his Elders (Gichi-Anishinaabe); they, in turn, wanted to honour him.

The Elders (Gichi-Anishinaabe) decided the young man (oshki-inini) should be buried high on the mountain (wajiw), where he had spent much of his youth hunting and gathering for everyone's benefit.

The Elders Gichi-Anishinaabe) asked the hunters (giiyosew-man) to gather deer belly fur (wabishkadowe); it was considered the most valuable; the young man (oshki-inini) would be wrapped in a cocoon of deer belly fur (wabishkadowe) for his final journey.

When the day arrived, the young man's (oshki-inini)body was carried across the river and transported to the top of the mountain (wajiw).

A small grave was dug, and his mother (ogiin) wrapped her son in the cocoon of white deer belly fur (wabishkadowe); she placed his arrows, bow and knife tools at his side. More furs were placed on top, and he was covered with flat stones.

After many years, the Elders (Gichi-Anishinaabe) noticed nothing had grown on the top of the mountain where the young man (oshki-inini) was laid to rest.

The following spring, some local kids came running back to the village saying small trees were growing on top of the mountain (wajiw); they looked different than others.

As the seasons progressed, great trees emerged all over the mountain; they had broad leaves that rattled on the wind, its bark was a brilliant white.

In the end, the young man (oshki-inini), laid to rest in white deer belly fur (wabishkadowe), had gifted his people with the great white birch tree.

Its bark has been used to make stronger canoes, birch water buckets and easy fire (ishkode) starters.

Indian Corn (Anishinaabe Mandaaminaak)

Anishinaabe Mandaaminaak

Many years ago, a poor Ojibwe man lived with his wife and children in present-day southern Ontario. He was poor but not particularly good at gathering food for his family, and his children were too young to assist him. Although poor, he was a man of a kind and contented disposition. He was always thankful to the Gichi Manitou for everything he received.

The same disposition was inherited by his eldest son, who had now arrived at the proper age to undertake the ceremony of fasting (gii'igoshimowin) to see what kind of a spirit his guide and guardian through life would be. For this was his name, Kunze had been an obedient boy from infancy and was of a reflective, thoughtful, and mild disposition, so he was beloved by the whole family.

As soon as the first indications of spring appeared, they built him the customary little wiigiwaam at a retired spot some distance from their own, where he would not be disturbed during this solemn rite. But, in the meantime, he prepared himself and immediately went into it and commenced fasting (gii'igoshimowin).

The first few days, he amused himself in the mornings by walking in the woods and over the mountains (wajiw), examining the early plants and flowers, and in this way, prepared himself to enjoy his sleep and, at the same time, stored his mind with pleasant ideas for his dreams. But, while he rambled through the woods, he felt a strong desire to know how the plants, herbs, and berries grew without any aid from man and why it was that some species were suitable to eat and others possessed medicinal or poisonous juices.

He recalled these thoughts to mind after becoming too tired to walk about and confined himself strictly to the lodge (wiigiwaam); he wished he could dream of something that would benefit his father, family, and others. "True!" he thought, "the Gichi Manitou made all things, and it is to him that we owe our lives.

But could he not make it easier for us to get food than hunting animals and taking fish? I must try to find out this in my visions."

He became weak and faint on the third day and kept his bed. While lying, he fancied seeing a handsome young man descending from the sky and advancing toward him. He was richly and gaily dressed, with great green and yellow colours differing in their deeper or lighter shades. He had a plume of waving feathers on his head, and all his motions were graceful.

"I am sent to you, my friend," said the celestial visitor, "by that Great Spirit (Gichi Manitou), who made all things in the sky and on the earth. He has seen and knows your motives in gii'igoshimowin. He sees that it is from a kind and benevolent wish to do good to your people and to procure a benefit for them and that you do not seek strength in war or the praise of warriors. Therefore, I am sent to instruct you and show you how you can do your kindred good."

He then told the young man to arise and prepare to wrestle with him, as it was only by this means that he could hope to succeed in his wishes. Kunze knew he was weak from gii'igoshimowin, but he felt his courage rising in his heart and immediately got up, determined to die rather than fail.

He commenced the trial and, after a protracted effort, was almost exhausted when the beautiful stranger said, "My friend, it is enough for once; I will come again to try you," and, smiling at him, he ascended in the air in the same direction from which he came.

The next day the celestial visitor reappeared at the same hour and renewed the trial. Kunze felt his strength was even less than the day before, but his mind's courage seemed to increase in proportion as his body became weaker. Seeing this, the stranger again spoke to him in the exact words he had used before, adding, "Tomorrow will be your last trial.

Be strong, my friend, for this is the only way to overcome me and obtain the boon you seek." On the third day, he again appeared at the same time and renewed the struggle. The poor youth was faint in body but grew more substantial in mind at every contest and was determined to prevail or perish in the attempt. He exerted his utmost powers, and after the game continued the usual time, the stranger ceased his efforts and declared himself conquered.

For the first time, he entered the wiigiwaam and sat down beside the youth, and he began to deliver his instructions to him, telling him how he should proceed to take advantage of his victory.

"You have won your desires of the Gichi Manitou," said the stranger. "You have wrestled manfully. Tomorrow will be the seventh day of your gii'igoshimowin. Your father will give you food to strengthen you, and as it is the last day of trial, you will prevail. I know this, and now tell you what you must do to benefit your family and tribe.

Tomorrow," he repeated, "I shall meet you and wrestle with you for the last time, and as soon as you have prevailed against me, you will strip off my garments and throw me down, clean the earth of roots and weeds, make it soft, and bury me in the spot.

When you have done this, leave my body in the earth, and do not disturb it, but come occasionally to visit the place, to see whether I have come to life, and be careful never to let the grass or weeds grow on my grave.

Once a month, cover me with fresh earth. If you follow my

instructions, you will accomplish your object of doing good to your fellow creatures by teaching them the knowledge I now teach you." He then shook him by the hand and disappeared.

In the morning, the youth's father came with some slight refreshments, saying, "My son, you have fasted long enough. If the Gichi Manitou favours you, he will do it now. It is seven days since you have tasted the food, and you must not sacrifice your life.

The Master of Life does not require that." "My father," replied the youth, "wait till the sun goes down. I have a particular reason for extending my fast to that hour." "Very well," said the old man, "I shall wait till the hour arrives and you feel inclined to eat."

At the usual hour of the day, the sky visitor returned, and the trial of strength was renewed. Although the youth had not availed himself of his father's food offer, he felt that new power had been given to him and that exertion had renewed his strength and fortified his courage.

He grasped his angelic antagonist with supernatural strength, threw him down, took from him his beautiful garments and plume, and, finding him dead, immediately buried him on the spot, taking all the precautions he had been told of and being very confident, at the same time, that his friend would again come to life.

He then returned to his father's wiigiwaam and partook sparingly of the meal prepared for him. But he never, for a moment, forgot the grave of his friend.

He carefully visited it throughout the spring, weeded the grass, and kept the ground soft and pliant. Very soon, he saw the tops of the green plumes coming through the floor, and the more careful he was to obey his instructions in keeping the ground in order, the faster they grew.

He was, however, careful to conceal the exploit from his father. Days and weeks had passed in this way. The summer was now drawing closer when one day, after a long absence in hunting, Kunze invited his father to follow him to the quiet and lonesome spot of his former fast. The wiigiwaam had been removed, and the weeds kept from growing on the circle where it stood, but in its place stood a tall and graceful plant with bright-coloured silken hair, surmounted with nodding plumes and stately leaves and golden clusters on each side. "It is my friend," shouted the lad; "it is the friend of all humankind. It is mandaaminaak (the name for corn).

We need no longer rely on hunting alone; as long as this gift is cherished and taken care of, the ground itself will give us a living." He then pulled an ear. "See, my father," said he, "this is what I fasted for. The Great Spirit (Gichi Manitou) has listened to my voice and sent us something new, and subsequently, our people will not alone depend upon the chase or the waters."

He then communicated to his father the instructions given to him by the stranger. First, he told him that the broad husks must be torn away, as he had pulled off the garments in his wrestling, and having done this, directed him how the ear must be held before the fire till the outer skin became brown milk was retained in the grain. The whole family then united in a feast on the newly grown ears, expressing gratitude to the Merciful Spirit who gave it.

So corn came into the world and has ever since been preserved.

Reprinted with Ojibwe translations by Richard Nanawin

SCHOOLCRAFT, H. R. (1839). *Algic researches. Open Library.*
https://openlibrary.org/works/OL1555053W/Algic_researches?edition=algicresearches00schogoog

How the Turtle (Mishekae) got its Shell

Mishekae

One lazy day, Nanabush was in a strange mood. He was woken up from his slumber by two noisy quarreling blue jays. Besides being woken up, he was hungry and decided to go to the village to find something to eat. When he arrived at the river's edge, he discovered two men cooking fish over a fire; he asked if he could have some.

The men gladly offered Nanabush a portion but warned him it would be scorching. Being very hungry and not heeding their warning, Nanabush grabbed the cooked fish (giigooh) with his bare hand and promptly burnt his hand.

In pain, he dropped the fish and ran towards the river, not looking where he was going. Suddenly, he tripped over a stone and fell on a Turtle (mishekae) who was sunning herself on the river's edge. Turtle (Mishekae) did not have a shell a long time ago. Instead, she had a long slender body with soft skin.

Turtle (Mishekae) yelled at Nanabush to watch where he was going. Nanabush felt terrible and apologized for his haste and clumsiness. But, Nanabush pondered, what could he do for the mishekae to help his friend stay safe from harm?

A little while later, Nanabush returned to the river's edge and called out to Turtle (Mishekae). She poked her head up through the soft sand. Nanabush picked up two large shells and placed them on top of each other. Then, he picked up the Turtle (Mishekae) and placed her between the shells. Nanabush said, "You'll never be hurt again. When danger comes upon you, you can retreat into your shell, head, legs and all".

As time passed by, the Turtle (Mishekae) outgrew her shells. Nanabush took some river clay and added shells to cover her body as she grew to adulthood. Nanabush mused. He said," Your surface itself is round like mother earth. Your hump reminds us of the hill and mountains; your four legs point in four directions, North, South, East and West.

Your tail will show the many lands the Anishnabek have been to, and your head will show the direction to follow to new lands. Each of the shells represents the different Anishnabek people who live across mother earth and are all part of the same family."

To this day, Anishinaabe refers to North America as Mishekae Island. This is because her many Nations are joined as one family in all four directions.

Nanabush Gets Power from the Skunk (Shaagaak)

Shaagaak

Hunting with a bow and tracking game was too much work for Nanabush. He believed there had to be an easier way. Skunk (Shaagaak) always had plenty of food. They did not seem to work too hard. If only I could hunt like him, I thought Nanabush. So, he tracked down Skunk (Shaagaak).

You are a great hunter, wise and strong. Teach me to hunt like you, and I'll be your friend forever, said Nanabush. But, of course, Nanabush did not mean a word he said. But Skunk (Shaagaak) needed a friend. So, he decided to give Nanabush some Skunk (Shaagaak) power.

Skunk (Shaagaak) power is excellent, no bows and arrows, no tracking games; life would be easy, though, Nanabush. But do not waste this great gift, warned Skunk (Shaagaak). Nanabush quickly agreed. Shaagaak gave Nanabush a flute and taught him a song.

Then he told Nanabush to build a lodge (wiigiwaam), sit inside, and play his flute and Caribou (Adik) would soon come dancing in. Only then was he to use his power to slay the Caribou (Adik), Nanabush agreed.

Skunk (Shaagaak) told Nanabush to kneel on all fours; he then backed up to him and filled Nanabush with Skunk's (Shaagaak's) magical power. Nanabush was highly excited and could not wait to get started. While looking for a place to build his lodge (wiigiwaam), Nanabush spotted a vast oak tree. He stared down the giant tree, then used his Skunk (Shaagaak) power and blasted it to splinters. Nanabush was incredibly pleased.

He found a good location and began work on his lodge (wiigiwaam). But a huge rock was in the way. No problem. Instead of walking around the boulder, Nanabush blew it out. His lodge (wiigiwaam) was soon finished. He sat and played his flute. To his amazement, Caribou (Adik) soon filled his home.

One blast and he would have enough meat for the winter! But nothing came out. He tried again and again until his face turned red. No more Skunk (Shaagaak) power! He sat and watched helplessly as the Caribou (Adik) scampered over him and into the bush, laughing loudly.

Nanabush cried," My food!" Then, he grabbed his bow and began chasing the fleeing Caribou (Adik).

Nanabush Creates the M'Chigeeng Bluffs

M'Chigeeng

Nanabush never missed an opportunity to play a trick. One day he saw the great water Snake (Ginebig) sleeping on the shore. So much too peaceful, thought Nanabush. Grandmother

(Nokomis) said, "Leave Snake (Ginebeg) alone! Let us go walk in the woods."

Of course, this gave Nanabush an idea. Snake (Ginebig) hates to be out of the water. So, using magic, he hung Snake (Ginebeg) high in the trees, deep in the woods, far from shore.

Then he poked Snake (Ginebeg) with a stick. Snake (Ginebeg) awoke suddenly, shocked to be high in the trees and far from his watery home. Nanabush laughed, long and loud.

Snake (Ginebeg) did not laugh. Instead, angrily he lunged at Nanabush. Nanabush jumped to avoid the attack, lifted Nokimis onto his back and ran off, believing Ginebeg would not chase them. But he did. And Ginebeg would not stop until Nanabush paid for his trickery.

With Grandmother (Nokomis) on his back, he ran day and night around all the great waters. Finally, Nanabush grew tired of carrying Grandmother (Nokomis). He rested on Manitoulin Island. He realized Snake (Ginebeg) would soon catch up, which would be trouble.

He had to leave his Grandmother (Nokomis), which saddened Nanabush. It was his responsibility to care for Grandmother (Nokomis); if he left her, Snake (Ginebeg) would kill her. So, he had to hide his Grandmother (Nokomis). So, he threw her into a nearby lake and changed her into a beautiful island we call Mindemoya, which means "old lady."

The island reminds us to look after our elderly, no matter what troubles are chasing us. With Grandmother (Nokomis) safely hidden, Nanabush started to run again. Finally, Nanabush stopped running, and Snake (Ginebeg) drew closer. Nanabush knew he would have to slay the Great Snake (Ginebeg).

He reached for his bow and arrow, but Nanabush, being as he

is, did not bother to finish his arrows. They had no arrowheads. He reached into his pocket and found an arrowhead. He fumbled with the head, trying desperately to ready his arrow. Snake (Ginebeg) crashed through the trees and was ready to strike.

Looking up, Nanabush quickly decided this was not the time to fight. He dropped his arrowhead and disappeared into the bush as Snake (Ginebeg) attacked. He struck Nanabush's arrowhead lying on the ground with such force it formed massive bluffs in the shape of an arrowhead.

These bluffs overlook our homes in M'Chigeeng and are called Mihigiwadmong to remind us of Nanabush's adventure.

The Fox (Waagosh) and the Bear (Makwa)

Makwa

Waagosh

One chilly fall day, Fox (Waagosh) was on the frozen lake fishing for food; he was watched closely by Bear (Makwa), who was on the shoreline looking through the tall grass.

He watched as Fox (Waagosh) used his sharp claws to dig a small hole through the ice; he watched intently as the Fox (Waagosh) took his big bushy tail (ozow) and plunged it through the hole into the icy lake water.

He watched as Fox (Waagosh) wriggled his big bushy tail (ozow) and shuffled around a couple of times; suddenly, Fox (Waagosh) pulled his big bushy tail (ozow) straight up; it was covered in Perch (Asaawe) that had a bit on to his big bushy tail (ozow).

Fox (Waagosh) walked a short way and slowly took each Perch (Asaawe) off his big bushy tail (ozow) and feasted on his catch. The Bear (Makwa) was intrigued; he was hungry and decided to cross the ice and take some of Fox (Waagosh's) fresh Perch (Asaawe).

Fox (Waagosh) did not notice the Bear (Makwa) coming onto the ice first, but he heard a large crack and boom as the Bear (Makwa) put his total weight on the ice. Before Fox (Waagosh) could run, Bear (Makwa) was too close to run around him; he just sat down and waited for Bear (Makwa) to take his fish.

Bear (Makwa) approached Fox (Waagosh), crouching on the ice, frozen in fear; Bear (Makwa) reached out and used his vast law to nab a Perch (Asaawe) and eat it without chewing. Fox (Waagosh) said, "You look hungry, Bear (Makwa); take them all; please let me go back to my brothers and sisters."

Bear (Makwa) ate all the Perch (Asaawe); he asked Fox (Waagosh) to catch more for him. Fox (Waagosh) said, "I must get home before dark; I will show you how to catch all the fish you can eat." Bear (Makwa) mused for a time, then said, "Okay, show me your secret, and I'll let you go back to brothers and sisters."

Fox (Waagosh) old Bear (Makwa), "You have to dig a hole in the ice, not too big but just big enough for your big bushy tail (ozow)." So bear (Makwa) took his massive paw and dug his long claws into the ice; a couple of sweeps, and he was, though; he pushed the ice aside.

Fox (Waagosh) told Bear (Makwa) to take his big bushy tail (ozow), plunge it down into the hole in the ice and wiggle it around. Bear (Makwa) had seen Fox (Waagosh) do the same; he looked forward to a Perch (Asaawe) feast of his very own.

Bear (Makwa) backed up to the ice hole and plunged his big bushy tail (ozow) into the icy water; he wiggled around and waited. Just then, he could feel something biting his big bushy tail (ozow), then another and another; Bear (Makwa) was getting excited. Finally, Fox (Waagosh) said, "Wait a bit longer, wait for big bushy tail (ozow) to become heavy." Bear (Makwa) waited just like Fox (Waagosh) had said; his tale was getting heavy.

Bear (Makwa) suddenly stood up, his big bushy tail (ozow) flew out of the icy water covered in fresh Peach (Asaawe), " You were right, Fox (Waagosh), I have plenty of Peach (Asaawe) to feast upon; go home to your brothers and sisters."

Bear (Makwa) sat down the icy hole; he took the Peach (Asaawe) off his big bushy tail (ozow) and started to feast on the Perch (Asaawe); one, two, three, seven ….10, 11, he was eating as fast as possible. Bear (Makwa) finished all his first catch, but he was still hungry, he decided to fish for more Perch (Asaawe).

Bear (Makwa) plunged his big bushy tail (ozow) back into the icy hole; before long, he had lots of Perch (Asaawe) biting onto his big bushy tail (ozow); he jumped up and put his big bushy tail (ozow) out of the water. After that, bear (Makwa) settled down and ate all the Perch (Asaawe) he had caught; it was getting darker, but Bear (Makwa) was greedy; he wanted more Perch (Asaawe).

Bear (Makwa) took his big bushy tail (ozow) and plunged once more into the icy hole, he wiggled around, but he was getting tired. He's eaten so much and was getting full; he decided to stop wiggling his big bushy tail (ozow) and rest.

The sunset came, and Bear (Makwa) was so full of Perch (Asaawe); he fell asleep sitting with this big bushy tail (ozow) in the icy hole. Later, early in the morning, Fox (Waagosh) returned to the frozen lake; he saw Bear (Makwa) sitting and sleeping on the ice. Fox (Waagosh) approached carefully; he yelled, " Bear (Makwa), Bear (Makwa), wake up, wake up !!" Bear (Makwa) woke up. "What do you want, Fox (Waagosh)?" Fox (Waagosh) told Bear (Makwa) he had fallen asleep on the ice; it was morning

Bear (Makwa) tried to get up, but he was stuck to the ice;

he pulled harder and harder, and his big bushy tail (ozow) was frozen. Fox (Waagosh) encouraged Bear (Makwa) to pull harder; the ice was cracking but not releasing his big bushy tail (ozow).

Bear (Makwa) gave one more big pull; he heard a crack, then a pop; it was free, but when he looked back, his big bushy tail (ozow) was still stuck in the ice.

So, to this day, Makwa has a short little bushy tail (ozow).

Nanabush and Dog (Animosh)

Animosh

One night an exceptionally long time ago, Nanabush tended to his fire and settled down in his lodge (wiigiwaam) for a good night's rest. He had added a few extra pieces of wood to his fire; he knew the nights were starting to get colder as winter winds approached.

Nanabush crawled into bed, closed his eyes, and let his mind wander about tomorrow's adventures; all was quiet until the village dogs decided to gather on the hill under the full moon.

All the Dogs (Animosh) had gathered on the hill overlooking Nanabush's village; they began howling, barking, and running around under the full moon. Nanabush tried to ignore the barking, and how; the longer he tried, the louder they got; he had finally had enough.

Nanabush got out of bed and made his way in the dark up the hill towards the Dogs (Animosh); he could hear them getting louder and louder as he approached. When he got to the top of the hill, he saw 20 or 30 Dogs (Animosh) of all colours and shapes running and jumping: barking and howling at the full moon.

Nanabush decided it was time to chase them away; he took a big breath of air and began to yell, "Go home!! Get!! Go Home, you Dogs (Animosh)!!". The Dogs (Animosh) all looked startled; they took off in all directions running down the hill toward the village; Nanabush was happy. It was quiet again.

Nanabush took his time walking back to his lodge (wiigiwaam); he enjoyed the fresh air, the full moon and, exceptionally, the quiet. When he arrived at his lodge (wiigiwaam), he noticed many Dog (Animosh) tails of all shapes and colours lying by the entrance; he walked towards his fire and found the Dogs (Animosh) he had chased away.

They were all curled up around his fire, and all were sleeping; it was noticeably quiet. Nanabush decided they could stay if they were silent; he returned to his bed and laid down for a good night's rest. As he lay there, his nose began to twitch; he could smell something; it stunk bad; he tried to ignore it for a while but to no avail.

Nanabush got up and walked towards his fire; the stink got stronger; it was the Dogs (Animosh); they had gotten some rotten fish guts on their fur. Nanabush decided he would not get any sleep with the foul smell in his lodge (wiigiwaam). Nanabush took a deep breath and yelled," Get out, you stinky Dogs (Animosh), take your smell with you, Go!!".

All the Dogs (Animosh) jumped up and took off for the door, grabbing their tails on the way out. Finally, Nanabush was satisfied; he could sleep with no stink noise this night.

Something happened that night when the Dogs (Animosh) took off and grabbed their tails; they had grabbed the wrong tails.

When Dogs (Animosh) greet each other today, they sniff each other's tails, looking for the tail they lost in all the confusion.

Why People (Anishinaabe) do not live forever

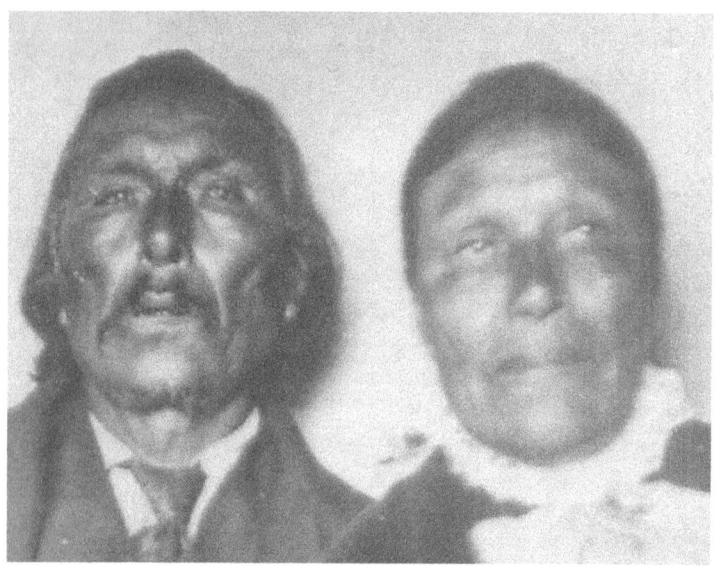

Aanikoobijigan (Jacob and Sarah Nanawin)

Nanabush always wanted to help people; he travelled from village to village, helping all Turtle Island people and animals.

He lived close to his Grandmother (Nokimos) for a long time but lived alone in his lodge (wiigwaam), never taking a partner. As the years passed, Nanabush became restless; he was unhappy; he had done much for all the creatures of Turtle Island.

One night, Nanabush was sleeping in his lodge (wiigiwaam) he heard a voice speaking to him. Was it a dream or real? "Who's there? He asked aloud.

Just then, he realized it was the creator Great Spirit (Gitchi Manitou) speaking to him; he listened very carefully.

Great Spirit (Gitchi Manitou) told Nanabush, "Rest well tonight; in the morning, you will journey to the east towards the rising sun and find a fast-moving river. When you get to the water's edge, do not hesitate; walk upon the water; it will hold you. Then, on the far shore, you find something you have desired for a long time".

In the morning awoke, he put on his moccasins, packed some dried meat, and set off to begin his journey as Great Spirit (Gitchi Manitou) had instructed him. Nanabush knew his territory well, but this journey took him beyond the area he knew; he continued to walk towards the rising, looking for the great river.

Nanabush travelled across many creeks; he had walked for many hours; the sun was now high in the middle of the sky; it was getting sweltering. Nanabush suddenly realized he could smell watery mist and hear rushing water; as he came through the trees, there was the mighty river in front of him.

The river was angry and foaming violently; it splashed over Nanabush as he jumped upon the high boulders above the raging river. Nanabush was terrified; if he entered the water, the whirlpools and rapids would surely take him under, and he would drown. But, as he stood there, he remembered what

Great Spirit (Gitchi Manitou) had said, "Do not hesitate, walk upon the water"; Nanabush looked across the raging river, and there he saw a beautiful woman smiling back at him the opposite shore.

Nanabush to a few quick steps upon the water; the water held him up just like a soft forest floor of moss; the moccasins were repealing the water. Nanabush crossed the river carefully. Once he arrived on the far shore, the beautiful woman embraced him and said. "I am your wife; Great Spirit (Gitchi Manitou) sent me to be your life partner."

Nanabush was incredibly happy; all the years of loneliness had washed away; he embraced her and imagined a family of children around him just like all the other creatures of Turtle Island.

Nanabush and his wife settled down by the river where they had first met; they had many children; their children would grow and flourish; these would become the first Ojibwe people.

As the years passed, Nanabush watched as his children grew to become parents and grandparents of their own; strangely, they did not stop aging like Nanabush and his wife. Nanabush was happy; he knew his last days among the people of Turtle Island would soon come. Great Spirit (Gitchi Manitou) spoke the Nanabush. "It is time for you and your wife to join the Land of the Spirit people, follow the west wind."

To this day, the Ojibwe people of Turtle Island do not live forever because Nanabush hesitated at the great river's edge and did not listen to Gitchi Manitou's words.

Nanabush and Rude Eagle (Migizi)

Migizi

One season, Nanabush was another one of his adventures into a neighbouring territory that he was unfamiliar with; he did not know where he was. So he decided to ask the first animal he came across where he was; he suddenly heard flapping wings as a great Eagle (Migizi) took off from a high treetop.

He yelled out loudly to the Eagle (Migizi) several times; the

Eagle (Migizi) looked down and ignored Nanabush's calls; this angered Nanabush. So Nanabush transformed into a great Eagle (Migizi) and set off after the rude Eagle (Migizi) that had ignored him.

Nanabush had transformed into a mighty Eagle (Migizi) with large wings and a sharpened, dangerous hooked beak; he flew high into the sky and pursued the Eagle (Migizi) that ignored him.

The Eagle (Migizi) spotted Nanabush flying up towards him; he decided to fly higher and higher through the clouds into the blazing sunshine (giizis).

Higher and higher they flew, Nanabush giving chase. The air was getting hotter and hotter. As they flew higher and higher, they were getting close to the sun itself; the Eagle (Migizi) would not let Nanabush catch him.

The Eagle (Migizi) suddenly became confused; his eyes began to burn, and he closed them; the sun scorched and burned off his head feathers; Nanabush saw this, flew above the Eagle (Migizi) and pushed him away from the sun towards the ground.

As the Eagle (Migizi) regained his senses, the ground was approaching fast; he prepared to land safely; just then, Nanabush swooped under him and prevented him from landing.

Nanabush said, " You and your children will be punished for ignoring my words; you will never be able to grow proper feathers on your head nor land safely on solid ground; if you do, you will be in great danger from other animals."

To this day, Ojibwe people refer to the Eagle (Migizi) as a bald Eagle (Migizi) and rarely see them land on the ground.

Nanabush and the Woodpecker (Baapaase)

Baapaase

Nanabush decided to go for a walk in the forest; he was hungry and needed dinner. While walking along the edge of the forest, he heard animals growling and snarly in the open meadow; he decided to sneak up and look. To his surprise, he saw two bears (Makwa's) fighting over fresh-killed meat. Finally, Nanabush thought, this was his chance; he would not have to hunt for his dinner; he jumped from the trees and began running towards the two bears (Makwa's), waving his arms and yelling.

The two bears (Makwa's) were surprised to see Nanabush running towards them, yelling and shaking his arms; they took one last bite and took off for the nearby forest. Nanabush was proud of himself; he did not have to hunt tonight; he took the meat, threw it over his shoulder and walked back to his lodge (wiigiwaam). He carved about half the meat for a meal and hid the rest in a hiding place in his lodge (wiigiwaam)

While the meat was cooked, Nanabush decided to go for another walk and look for wild onions and mushrooms for his meal. All the noise and commotion had attracted other animals in the forest; two wolves watched as Nanabush walked right of them, singing a song to himself. As Nanabush walked in the opposite direction, the Wolves (Ma'iingan) could smell the meat cooking that Nanabush had left behind. The Wolves (Ma'iingan) went into Nanabush's lodge (wiigiwaam), tore the meat from the fire and had a great feast; they sniffed out the hidden meat and ate that as well before leaving with full stomachs.

Nanabush returned to find his dinner had been stolen along with the meat he had hidden for another meal. He was angry; he would find out who took his food and punish them; however, Nanabush had no idea who stole it; besides, the Wolves (Ma'iingan) were long gone without a trace.

It was too late to hunt; Nanabush decided to search out his

friend, the great Woodpecker (Baapaase); he would likely eat dinner soon. So Nanabush walked for a while and finally came to the camp of the great Woodpecker (Baapaase)," Hello, my friend, I have come to talk."

The great Woodpecker (Baapaase) looked down from his perch and flew down to join Nanabush by the fire pit. Nanabush told the great Woodpecker (Baapaase) what had happened to his dinner and how it was stolen from his lodge (wiigiwaam.) The great Woodpecker (Baapaase) felt sorry for Nanabush; he said, "I will get us dinner. Do you like a Raccoon (Esiban)?".

Nanabush jumped to his feet," Can I help? The great Woodpecker (Baapaase) said, "No, I will get our dinner myself." So the great Woodpecker (Baapaase) walked into his lodge (wiigiwaam) and emerged with two long narrow pieces of bone; he inserted one in each nostril.

He flew up to a nearby tree and began to tap the bark with the bone pins; suddenly, one Raccoon (Esiban) fell out of the branches crashing to the ground below, followed by another.

The great Woodpecker (Baapaase) roasted the Raccoons (Esiban) for dinner; both sat down and ate a great feast. Nanabush was very thankful for the meal; he said, "I will repay your kindness soon; I will hunt for you and invite you for a feast."

A few weeks later, Nanabush decided to hunt like the great Woodpecker (Baapaase); he fashioned two sharp wooden pegs and pushed them up to his nose. Then, he climbed a nearby Pine tree like a great Woodpecker (Baapaase). Then, he began to tap the tree with the wooden pegs. While he was up the Pine tree, the great Woodpecker (Baapaase) arrived for dinner; he noticed Nanabush high up in the Pine tree.

The great Woodpecker (Baapaase) laughed to himself;

Nanabush doesn't know great Woodpecker (Baapaase) magic to hunt Raccoons (Esiban). So the great Woodpecker (Baapaase) decided to let Nanabush try, but he knew he would have to chase the Raccoon (Esiban) himself.

Suddenly, Nanabush lost his grip on the pine tree and fell to the earth with a great crash; the fall knocked him out; he was bleeding badly from his nose. The great Woodpecker (Baapaase) lifted Nanabush off the ground, propped him up against a nearby tree and stopped the bleeding. Then, the great Woodpecker (Baapaase) took the wooden pegs out of the Nanabush's nostrils and set off to hunt Raccoon (Esiban) with his bone pegs.

He soon returned and put the Raccoons (Esiban)on to roast; he shook Nanabush and came around and smelled the Raccoon (Esiban) roast. Then, the great Woodpecker (Baapaase) said, "Silly Nanabush, you can't use great Woodpecker (Baapaase) magic for hunting Raccoons (Esiban); it's a secret."

Nanabush smiled weakly, "I am very grateful to you, great Woodpecker (Baapaase); I want everyone to remember your kindness." Then, Nanabush took some of his bright red blood and wiped it on great Woodpecker (Baapaase) chest feathers and some on his head feathers, "Wear my bright red blood as your reward; your children will all be emboldened and know your kindness."

Today, all great Woodpeckers (Baapaase) have a red crest on their chest and heads.

The Great Spirit (Gitchi Manitou), the Rabbit (Waabooz) and the Owl (Gookooko'oo)

Waabooz

Gookooko'oo

One day, the Great Spirit (Gitchi Manitou), the creator, was making animals for Turtle Island. Rabbit (Waabooz) said. "I want strong, powerful legs like Deer and big ears so I can hear better than all the other animals; I want razor shape teeth and claws like the forest cats."

Great Spirit (Gitchi Manitou) was generous; he always listened to the animals; he tried his best to make Rabbit's (Wabooz) legs long and strong, just like he would ask. Not too far away, Owl was sitting in a tree waiting for his turn, "Whoooo!! Whoooo!!, I want a long neck like a Crane, bright feathers like the great Woodpecker (Baapasse) and a great beak like the Eagle (Migizi). I want to be beautiful and fly as fast as a falcon!!".

"Be quiet!!" said Great Spirit (Gitchi Manitou), "You are

forbidden to watch me work, turn around and close your eyes.

Owl was stubborn, "You can't tell me to stop looking at you, turn around or close my eyes; I'm going to sit here because I can."

This angered Great Spirit (Gitchi Manitou); he dropped Rabbit (Wabooz) and grabbed Owl from the tree. He pushed Owl's head down deep into his chest. He shook Owl until his eyes popped open in fear and pulled owls ears out the side of his head.

"That will teach you, Owl!!, You won't be able to crane your head to watch things that are not your concern. Your big ears will hear everything, especially when someone is telling you not to bother them; your feathers with not be bright or colourful. They will be grey like mud. Your eyes are too big for the daytime. You will sleep during the day and be wide awake all night. This will be your punishment for not listening to me".

Owl was resigned to his fate for not listening Great Spirit (Gitchi Manitou); he flew away into the dark forest pouting. Great Spirit (Gitchi Manitou) turned back to finish his work on Wabooz, but alas, Wabooz was so scared he took off running unfinished.

To this day, Wabooz is unfinished; his back legs are long and powerful, and his front legs are short; he must hop everywhere.

After being so frightened, Wabooz trusts no one and is very wary of all who approach them. Had he not run away, he would be very different indeed.

Nanabush and the Great Beaver (Amik)

Amik

Nanabush did not always get along with all the animals of Turtle Island; one formidable foe was the great Beaver (Amik). Nanabush chased the great Beaver (Amik) for an exceptionally long time across rivers, through swamps and lakes; the great Beaver (Amik) was a clever adversary; he had magical powers that he used to escape from Nanabush.

Nanabush was still living with his Grandmother (Nokomis)) when this story took place; despite her age, she helped Nanabush track the great Beaver (Amik) for a long time; they eventually became disheartened when they lost track of him at the edge of a great lake. (Lake Superior).

The chase had brought them to the edge of their territory; they were both tired; Nanabush set to building a new lodge (wiigiwaam); there were lots of large white birch near the shore of the great lake that could be stitched together for their new temporary home. In the following weeks, Grandmother (Nokomis)) would spend her days fishing while Nanabush hunted in the nearby forest.

A few weeks later, Nanabush noticed the shoreline had changed; the lake water had risen several inches and was now awfully close to his fire pit. Nanabush was curious to determine what was causing the level change; he set out towards the rising sun in the eastern sky. As he walked the shoreline, he saw the lake narrowing; cliffs on each side; just then, he saw the great Beaver (Amik) had gathered lots of trees; he was building a dam at the narrows.

Now that Nanabush why the water was rising, he ran back to Grandmother (Nokomis) to tell her he had found the great Beaver building a dam. So Nanabush brought Grandmother (Nokomis) to the dam's site; the great Beaver (Amik) had been busy, the dam was almost sealed, and the great Beaver (Amik) was nowhere to be seen.

Nanabush makes a plan, Grandmother (Nokomis) would sit atop the dam and wait for the great Beaver (Amik) to return; Nanabush would walk the shore of the next lake (Lake Huron) and chase the great Beaver (Amik) back toward the dam. "My journey may take a few days; you must stay awake and not let his escape,' said Nanabush; his Grandmother (Nokomis) sat upon the highest point as she watched Nanabush begin his journey along the lake shore.

Grandmother (Nokomis) watched the sunset in the west and

watched it rise again in the east; she was tired but knew she must stay awake just if the great Beaver (Amik) returned; another day passed by, and the sun was setting once again with no sign of the great Beaver (Amik) on the horizon. Finally, as the blue light of the second morning lit up the sky, Grandmother (Nokomis) caught herself nodding and falling asleep; she fought to keep her eyes open.

Suddenly, Grandmother (Nokomis) heard a splash close by; she peered over the dam and saw the great Beaver (Amik) making his way out of the water. Just then, the great Beaver (Amik) spotted Grandmother (Nokomis) above him, he tried to turn and escape, but Grandmother (Nokomis) reached out with her hands and grabbed the great Beaver (Amiks) tail.

The great Beaver (Amik) fought to free his tail; he thrashed back and forth and clawed at his dam but to no avail; Grandmother (Nokomis) had an iron grip on the great Beaver (Amik)s tail. While Grandmother (Nokomis) hung on, she yelled out for Nanabush, hoping he was nearby and could help her drag the great Beaver (Amik) from the water.

The great Beaver (Amik) realized old Grandmother (Nokomis) would not let go; she did not have the strength to pull him out of the water. So the great Beaver (Amik) decided he must escape before Nanabush returns; he looked around and came up with a cunning plan. The great Beaver (Amik) spun around and began to dig into the side of the dam he had built; trees, branches, mud, and leaves began to fall into the water below. Many hours passed; Grandmother (Nokomis) could see what the great Beaver (Amik) was up to; she called out to Nanabush, all the while the great Beaver (Amik) dug into his own dam.

There was no sign Nanabush, Grandmother (Nokomis)

refused to let go of the great Beaver (Amik)s tail; suddenly, water began to seep under the feet of Grandmother (Nokomis), and her moccasins were getting wet. Big deep cracking sounds could be heard, the dam began to vibrate and finally with a great Whoosh!!!!!!! The dam began to collapse upon itself. Grandmother (Nokomis) let go of the great Beaver (Amik) tail and jumped back on the nearby boulders to avoid being sweep away; the great Beaver (Amik) was caught up in their destruction; he managed to hang on to a log sweep out of sight through the narrow rapids.

Grandmother (Nokomis) sat on the nearby shore; she was tired and sore, she had fought well, but the great cunning Beaver (Amik) had destroyed his own house to save himself. She gazed out upon Lake Huron; she could see the great Beaver (Amik) many miles away, sunning himself under the cliffs above.

Much of the great Beaver (Amik) dams were washed away, but many trees, mud and branches had gotten caught between the narrow forming new islands. This would become today Thirty Thousand Island between Lake Superior and Lake Huron.

Nanabush eventually returned; he had heard the great crash as the dam collapsed; he took to higher ground to avoid being sweep away by the surge of water. He reached out and hugged his Grandmother (Nokomis) and said," the great Beaver (Amik) is a cunning and dangerous foe; we will follow his new trail after you rest awhile."

Nanabush and Grandmother (Nokomis) continued to track the great Beaver (Amik) for months; they crossed Lake Huron, Lake St Clair, and Lake Erie; they pressed on until they came to the mouth of a great river emptying in the great east ocean. The great river was the St. Lawrence River, where it meets the great eastern Atlantic Ocean; Nanabush and Grandmother

(Nokomis) stood on the shore; neither could see the far shore; the ocean was vast.

Just when they decided to return to the north country, Grandmother (Nokomis) saw the great ocean rise and fall; then, she saw the great Beaver (Amik)s head rise above the surface. Nanabush and Grandmother (Nokomis) were amazed; the great Beaver (Amik) had gone to the edge of Turtle Island to avoid capture; he was stubborn and cunning, Nanabush decided he would no longer hunt the great Beaver (Amik).

Nanabush called out to the great Beaver (Amik), 'Come back, come back, you've bested Grandmother (Nokomis) and me, let us be friends!!!"

The great Beaver (Amik) swam to shore; he feasted with Nanabush and Grandmother (Nokomis). They told stories and recounted their adventurous chase through the eastern lakes to the great ocean. Finally, the great Beaver (Amik) returned to the north country; he had many offspring who became the great Beaver (Amik) we know today, though a lot smaller but just as industrious as their great ancestor.

About the Author

Richard is Anishinaabe Aadizookaan (A traditional storyteller); he has shared his stories of Nanabush and his adventures with countless children and adults on Turtle Island. Richard Nanawin was born in 1965, a Traditional Ojibwe/Cree Storyteller from Poplar River First Nation in northern Manitoba. His Ookomisan (grandmothers- grandmother) is Ojibwa/Cree from Poplar River First Nation, Manitoba; his Omishoomisan (grandfathers-grandmother) is Chippewa from Fond Du Lac Indian Nation, Michigan, USA.

www.ingramcontent.com/pod-product-compliance
Lightning Source LLC
Chambersburg PA
CBHW070303120526
44590CB00017B/2551